er

is it

# MOTIVATE
# PEOPLE

8

## Better Management Skills

This highly popular range of inexpensive paperbacks covers all areas of basic management. Practical, easy to read and instantly accessible, these guides will help managers to improve their business or communication skills. Those marked * are available on audio cassette.

The books in this series can be tailored to specific company requirements. For further details, please contact the publisher, Kogan Page, telephone 0171-278 0433, fax 0171-837 6348.

Be a Successful Supervisor
Business Etiquette
Coaching Your Employees
Counselling Your Staff
Creative Decision-making
Creative Thinking in Business
Delegating for Results
Effective Meeting Skills
Effective Performance
  Appraisals*
Effective Presentation Skills
Empowerment
First Time Supervisor
Get Organised!
Goals and Goal Setting
How to Communicate
  Effectively*
How to Develop a Positive
  Attitude*
How to Develop Assertiveness
How to Write a Staff Manual
How to Understand Financial
  Statements
Improving Employee
  Performance
Improving Relations at Work
Keeping Customers for Life
Leadership Skills for Women

Learning to Lead
Make Every Minute Count*
Managing Disagreement
  Constructively
Managing Organisational
  Change
Managing Part-Time Employees
Managing Quality Customer
  Service
Managing Your Boss
Marketing for Success
Memory Skills in Business
Mentoring
Office Management
Productive Planning
Project Management
Quality Customer Service
Rate Your Skills as a Manager
Sales Training Basics
Self-Managing Teams
Selling Professionally
Successful Negotiation
Successful Telephone Techniques
Systematic Problem-solving and
  Decision-making
Team Building
Training Methods that Work
The Woman Manager

# HOW TO MOTIVATE PEOPLE

## A Guide for Managers

### SECOND EDITION

## Twyla Dell

KOGAN
PAGE

To Carl Blomgren for his patience
and invaluable support

First published in the United States of America
in 1988 under the title *An Honest Day's Work*
by Crisp Publications Inc, 1200 Hamilton Court,
Menlo Park, California 94025, USA. Second Edition 1988.

This edition first published in Great Britain in 1989
by Kogan Page Ltd, 120 Pentonville Road, London N1 9JN
Reprinted 1990, 1991, 1992, 1993, 1994, 1995
Second edition 1995

**British Library Cataloguing in Publication Data**

A CIP record for this book is available from the British Library.

ISBN 0-7494-1823-0

Typeset by DP Photosetting, Aylesbury, Bucks
Printed and bound in Great Britain by
Clays Ltd, St Ives plc

# Contents

# Contents

# About This Book

*How to Motivate People* is not like most books. It has a self-study format that encourages the reader to become personally involved. Designed to be read with a pencil in hand, it has an abundance of exercises, activities, assessments and cases that invite participation.

The object of this book is to provide guidelines which will create working conditions that bring out the best in employees. Five steps are presented that will help you get the best from your people. Each step has a bonus section with special advice. Each also has a story of real people who are getting the best from their workers.

This book (and the other self-improvement titles listed at the front) can be used effectively in a number of ways. Here are some possibilities:

*Individual study.* Because the book is self-instructional, all that is needed is a quiet place, some time, and a pencil. By completing the activities and exercises, a reader should not only receive valuable feedback, but also take practical steps for self-improvement.

*Workshops and seminars.* This book is ideal for assigned reading prior to a workshop or seminar. With the basics in hand, the quality of participation will improve, and more time can be spent on concept extensions and applications during the programme. The book is also effective when it is distributed at the beginning of a session, and participants work through the contents.

*Open learning.* Books can be used by those unable to attend home office training sessions.

*How to Motivate People* is also available on audio cassette.

One thing is certain, even after it has been read, this book will be looked at – and thought about – again and again.

# To the Reader

Most people want to give their best and be their best at work. Work, *at its best*, is the play of adults. It should be fun, inspiring, rewarding and challenging. Too often it is not. Most organisations get in the way of the simple desire to do well and make it very complicated for people to give their best work. Obstacles of all kinds make work slow, boring, unnecessarily difficult, fragmented, repetitious and tedious.

This book will give you very simple ways to identify, judge and remove the obstacles to motivating people at work. It will explain what people want most in their jobs and how to give it to them if you are a manager of people or what to ask for if you yearn for a more open and rewarding workplace.

*How to Motivate People* deals with the very heart of people's desire to give their best. It goes to their feelings that need to be recognised and resolved in a positive, caring way. It gives you the information you need to empower yourself and others to create an open, positive environment in which people look for ways to excel because they know they'll be recognised for it.

I hope you'll be motivated by what you read here – motivated to fill the needs of others in a way that works for all, motivated to create an atmosphere of fun, excitement and even adventure, and most of all motivated to enjoy working. That's what motivating yourself and others at work is all about.

Twyla Dell

# Introduction

Motivating people to work is not as difficult as it sounds. People want to work hard and have a good time, give their best and be recognised for it. They want to work for companies that understand that and give them room to do it. Why, then, does it seem so hard to get people to do what we want?

What does a motivating workplace look like? Feel like? The answers lie in the following pages. They are a mix of analysing, problem solving, empowering and rewarding. Creating a motivating workplace takes a little of each of those. First, analyse where the problems are. Who or what is the obstacle? Apply some creative problem solving to change things, empower people to do the work and recognise them in meaningful ways. In a nutshell, that's motivation. Naturally, it's not all that easy, but it is simple. Let's not lose sight of the simplicity of creating a motivating workplace as we grapple with the complexity of today's work.

Empowering workers is an idea whose time has come. Instead of a manager controlling staff members we have eliminated many managers. Instead of the manager dispensing the information as needed, workers have access through computers to as much information as they can handle. We've eliminated managers and moved to self-directed workteams. Empowerment is a natural next step. What does empowerment mean? To judge, act and command. Read about it in detail in the new section in this edition.

And while we're empowering, let's start with the squeaky wheel – the difficult employee. The difficult employee is usually a symptom of other problems and a good place to analyse what's wrong so we can start to make things right.

# Part 1
# Close the Commitment Gap!

## Meet the difficult employee ①

Fortunately, difficult employees are a minority. Still, even a few can foster unhappiness and unrest. How do employees become 'difficult'?

Most employees don't start out like that. Most want to work hard. They want to satisfy their needs through work, to be secure, to belong, to win recognition, to enjoy their job and learn new skills.

But often what workers want from work is not what employers give them. Employers want a product or service produced with as little trouble and as much profit as possible. Since they are product or profit motivated, they sometimes pay too little attention to the real needs of their employees.

Without realising what they are doing, managers can create the kind of negative atmosphere that causes employees to become difficult.

When there is a 'them against us' atmosphere or when products, services, deadlines or profits are valued higher than an individual's potential and feelings, difficult employees will multiply. They come out of hiding when their basic human needs are not met.

People have long been considered expenses, while stock, work-in-progress, supplies and buildings are viewed on the balance sheet as assets. Smart employers are now beginning to realise that people are the assets. The other things are less important to the success of the organisation.

**When difficult employees act up**

Difficult employees are those who swim against the current. They are the ones who 'act out' their unhappiness by complaining, sloping off, stealing time and sometimes being destructive. They are often bright, creative people who find they can't express themselves the way they'd like to on the job.

Have you worked with people who:

☐ Want to think for themselves rather than be told what to do?
☐ Have ideas on how to organise and run things better?
☐ Get bored with repetitious work?
☐ Become unproductive when not challenged?
☐ Dislike working for disorganised managers?
☐ Are unhappy working at something when they don't see the final product?
☐ Come in late, leave early?
☐ Hate being left out of meetings they can contribute to?
☐ Want someone to listen when they have suggestions on how to do things better?
☐ Resent working with poor tools and equipment?
☐ Are not content to work without knowing the overall picture?
☐ Want to have a say in how things turn out?
☐ Insist on a variety of pace and tasks?
☐ Beg for more responsibility and authority?
☐ Want to break off and have some fun – maybe even outside the office?
☐ Push to learn new skills?
☐ Want to be recognised when they do good work?
☐ Hate it when you don't remember their names?

As you ticked the boxes, did you recognise any of your own behaviour patterns as either an employee or manager?

## Why employees don't get the job done!

Usually, there are three reasons people don't get the job done. Regardless of what reasons people give, the answer may be one of these three:

**1. They don't know how**

**2. Something or someone keeps them from it**

**3. They don't want to**

Of the three possibilities described above what could you do to improve productivity in your area? List specific actions below:

**They don't know how**
Do any of your employees need training? Who could benefit from training? (Be specific.)

*Name*                                                          *Training needed*

_____

_____

_____

_____

**Something or someone keeps them from it**
Are there obstacles in your area?

_____

_____

_____

_____

**They don't want to**
Do you know why not?

_Name_                                                    _Why?_

_____

_____

_____

_____

**Enter time theft**
What happens when people don't know how to do their job, can't
do their job because something is keeping them from it, or don't
want to do their job? The answer is that they don't work to their
potential. Instead they commit 'time crime'.

   Call it what you like, it is the disappearance of time at the
organisation's expense. Whether workers slow the work pace,
avoid carrying out tasks, look for another job in company time,
make private phone calls or any other activity that robs the
company of needed results, it is _time theft_.

   Not much has been written about time theft but it is a costly
problem – millions of productive hours are lost each year. Time
theft haunts every manager.

   How many kinds of time theft have you observed? Tick them
off below.

☐ Work flow is held up by other departments.
☐ Work flow within a department is held up.
☐ Too many or too few employees for amount of work.
☐ Low morale slows work.
☐ Negative attitude towards _____ slows down work.

- ☐ Extra time tacked on to breaks and/or lunch.
- ☐ Frequent trips to the wash room.
- ☐ Lengthy personal phone calls.
- ☐ Non job-related activities such as _____ take time.
- ☐ Laziness or procrastination created by _____ .
- ☐ Inefficient management.
- ☐ Other _____
- ☐ Other _____

## The commitment gap

If you could have highly motivated workers who work to their fullest potential while producing excellent quality and product, would you want that? Of course! This kind of work is called 'commitment'. Commitment of employees to the organisation's vision and values, to excellence and productivity, is every manager's dream.

The first step in achieving this happy state is to analyse and close the commitment gap. The commitment gap is the difference between the time people are paid for working and the amount of time actually spent in productive labour.

| Percentage of time worked* |
|---|
| 10   20   30   40   50   60   70   80   90   100 |

Circle the average amount of time you think those around you work in productive ways. Is there a gap between what you circled and 100 per cent? If so, you need to find ways to improve productivity.

---

* Don't confuse looking busy with productivity, creative avoidance with output, slowdown with potential output or sabotage with problem solving.

## Measure the productivity

What would be the *improvement in productivity* to you and your organisation if you could close the commitment gap? How many more hours of productive labour could you create?

INVESTMENT:

Number of employees × number of hours paid:

RETURN:

Number of employees × number of hours productively worked:

THE DIFFERENCE BETWEEN THE INVESTMENT AND THE RETURN IS THE COST TO YOUR ORGANISATION.

Is there untapped potential in your department?

## Open to growth

It is acknowledged that workers in the future will require more mental skills. Managing creative people demands more sensitivity. As people become better informed, they expect to be treated better at work.

Treating employees better means finding ways to get them excited about their jobs. When ways are implemented to do that, it will help to close the commitment gap. It isn't always easy to close the commitment gap, but it is possible. And the pay-off is well worth the effort. Liberating an employee's potential is like finding gold. You may have to dig for it, but it brings great rewards when discovered.

When employee satisfaction improves the commitment gap begins to close. The atmosphere of the organisation changes. Expectations become positive. The pace quickens, people act with vigour and purpose. Morale rises.

The following pages will provide some thoughts about how to close the commitment gap in your organisation.

## What makes employees happy?

Every worker wants to feel good about doing his or her job. That's called 'employee satisfaction'. Employee satisfaction is made up of several factors, but they can be related to *five levels of need* first described by a psychologist in the 1960s, Abraham Maslow. Maslow said that each person has the same needs and that we all spend each day satisfying one or more of those needs.

### We need to survive
Our most basic need is to survive. You might compare that to a cave man killing a rabbit and crawling into a cave to cook and eat it.

### We need security
The next need is security. The cave man may kill several rabbits, then roll a stone in front of the cave door to protect his assets.

### We need to belong
Soon the cave man may feel lonely. Since he has enough rabbit for today and tomorrow, he invites some other cave people whose company he enjoys to share with him. He has now satisfied the need for belonging.

### We need prestige
Once he has others around, he appoints himself chief. This satisfies his need for prestige.

### We need self-fulfilment
Finally, his group is secure enough to decorate the cave walls with paintings and dance and sing. He is praised for having made it all possible and has reached the level of self-fulfilment.

Maslow's hierarchy (illustrated on page 21) shows that all humans have the same basic needs. How are these needs satisfied in the average job? Put an 'X' on the level where you think you spend most of your time. Are you at the survival level or closer to

## Where are you on the ladder?

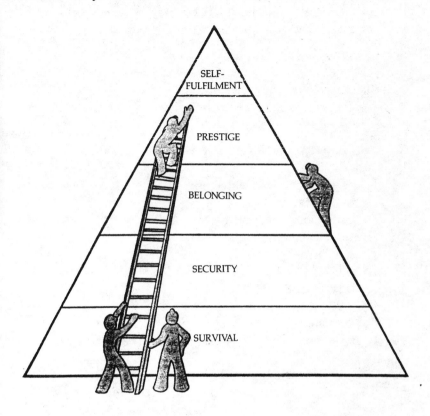

self-fulfilment? Or do you (like most people) operate mostly in the security or prestige levels?

Look again at the triangle. Circle your 'X' and then place new 'Xs' with the initials of others you work with, and where you think they fit.

## Ten qualities employees want in a job

Most organisations today are moving away from making people fit the job and towards making the job fit people. Jobs are becoming more flexible. Workplaces are becoming more responsive to workers' needs.

To attract and keep good people it will become increasingly necessary to create an atmosphere of learning and growth. This calls for a new kind of supervisor – one who can:

- coach
- teach
- lead employees to new challenges
- make people feel good about themselves
- keep individuals motivated and interested.

The following ten qualities are those that people want most from their jobs.

1. To work for efficient managers
2. To think for themselves
3. To see the end result of their work
4. To be assigned interesting work
5. To be informed
6. To be listened to
7. To be respected
8. To be recognised for their efforts
9. To be challenged
10. To have opportunities for increased skill development.

### Are you receiving the top ten?

How many of the ten qualities have you been *getting* in your job? To supervise others effectively, it helps if you are receiving what you need to give.

In the following exercise, rate yourself a 3 if you are satisfied with what you are *getting*. Give yourself a 2 if you are receiving an average amount of that quality. Rate yourself a 1 if the supply is scarce, and a 0 if you're not receiving any.

_____ I work for an efficient manager.

_____ I am encouraged to think for myself.

_____ I see the end result of my work.

_____ I have interesting work.

_____ I am listened to when I have ideas on how to do things better.

_____ I am informed about what is going on.

_____ I receive respect for my efforts.

_____ I am recognised for a job well done.

_____ I am challenged by what I do.

_____ I get opportunities for skill development.

_____ SCORE

A score of 24 or more means you're at the top of your ladder. A score of 15 to 23 suggests you're doing all right and can make some positive changes. A score of 8 to 14 indicates trouble; you may be a wage slave or simply filling in time. Put out your cv. 0 to 7 means you're falling off the ladder and need to seriously assess your career choice.

## Are you giving the top ten?

It's equally important to know how to _give_ the top ten qualities. It's easier to give them if you're receiving them. Even if that's not true, however, to get the most from your people and make your workplace the best it can be, you need to concentrate on giving as many of these qualities as possible.

Rate yourself again, this time on how much you're _giving_. Score a 3 for high, 2 for average, 1 for below average, 0 for not at all.

_____ I am an efficient manager.

_____ I encourage and teach employees to think for themselves.

_____ I arrange work so employees can see the end result.

_____ I divide work to make it as interesting as possible to everyone.

_____ I listen when there are ideas on how to do things better.

_____ I inform those who need to know about what is going on.

_____ I treat employees like professionals at all times.

_____ I recognise individuals for good work both formally and informally.

_____ I offer challenges whenever possible.

_____ I encourage skill development.

_____ SCORE

How did you score? 24 to 30 means you're an outstanding supervisor. 15 to 23 means you have the potential to be a leader. Keep practising. 8 to 14 says you're getting the picture but your workers are enduring in hopes of better days. 0 to 7, move aside and let someone else take over.

## Steps to improved productivity

It is interesting to note that the ten qualities employees want in a job described on page 22 match nicely with Maslow's five levels of need described on page 21. A manager sensitive to both Maslow's needs and the ten qualities employees want in a job is on the road to success. Some qualities fit several levels. For the purposes of this book, we have assigned qualities as shown below. The important thing is to learn how to deliver each quality effectively.

- The basic human need is *survival*. The core of employee satisfaction is to:
    1. Work for an efficient manager
    2. Think for oneself

- The next level of need is *security*. At this level employees need to:
    3. See the end result of their work
    4. Be involved in interesting work

- The third level of need is *belonging*. For belonging, employees need to:
    5. Be listened to
    6. Be informed

- The fourth level is *prestige*. For prestige, employees need:
    7. Respect
    8. Recognition

- The final level of need is *self-fulfilment*. At this level, employees need:
    9. A challenge
    10. Skill development

# Your one-page productivity plan

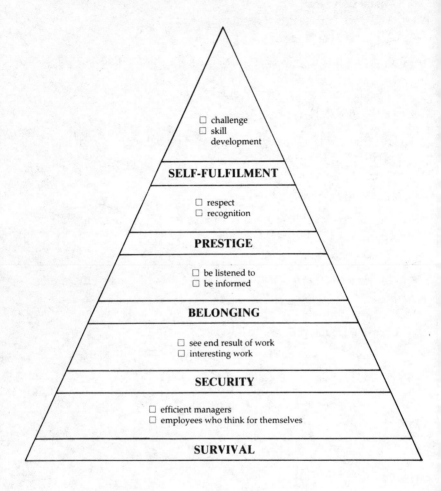

☐ challenge
☐ skill development

**SELF-FULFILMENT**

☐ respect
☐ recognition

**PRESTIGE**

☐ be listened to
☐ be informed

**BELONGING**

☐ see end result of work
☐ interesting work

**SECURITY**

☐ efficient managers
☐ employees who think for themselves

**SURVIVAL**

Start at the bottom and work your way up to become a 'top' manager.

# Part 2
# How to Empower Your Staff

A successful way to motivate employees in today's workplace is through empowerment. To empower means to give power and authority to someone. That power can be defined as the power to *judge, act* and *command.*

One of the most often used words in human resource development, empowerment became popular in the early 1980s. As the human resource movement grew, the understanding became clear that if our most important resource is our people, they need to be given access to growth and improvement. The only way they're going to grow is to be given more responsibility – the power to judge, act and command.

Empowerment is a condition wished for by both supervisors and employees. Yet creating a situation in which employees are empowered often feels threatening to the person in charge. On the one hand, empowerment sounds like a wonderful idea, what ought to happen in any forward-thinking organisation. On the other hand, concerns about deadlines, quality of work and control rear their heads. Is there a clear-cut definition of empowerment that gives a supervisor an understanding about empowering others? That's what this chapter is all about.

Obviously, the benefits of empowering others far outweigh concerns. Still, the process needs to be handled carefully. While these concerns are largely ungrounded, supervisors need to be aware of them and be *dedicated* to creating an empowering workplace. Above all, such concerns should not stop the move towards empowering people and building their leadership skills.

The benefits for everyone, including the organisation, are too great to lose.

What are the features and benefits of empowerment and what concerns do they raise?

| Features | Benefits | Concerns |
| --- | --- | --- |
| 1. Task is explained to employee and walked through process. | Employee learns new task, grows in skill. Someone is free to do other things. | Supervisor loses control. |
| 2. Task is given to employee to complete, make decisions, take responsibility. | Employee learns to carry out tasks unsupervised. | Employee won't do it right. ('I'll get blamed.') |
| 3. Employee repeatedly does task well. | Quality of work for company is repeated. | Employee will want more responsibility/ money or will get bored. |
| 4. Employee is given new tasks. | Loyalty, morale rises, productivity increases. | Supervisor or other person may be replaced. |

## The three phases of empowerment

A simple definition of empowerment is to give someone the power to:

1. judge
2. act
3. command

Too often employees are given the *direction* to act but don't have the *information* to judge or the *power* to command.

See the difference in these words? *Direction* is simply telling people what to do without their having the information to judge any changes along the path. Direction is dead-end instruction unless it also includes enough information to *judge* changes and surprises and *power* to get the results needed. Without judgement and power, the person has very little, if any, room to respond intelligently to unexpected changes.

Robots act. People judge and command. Without the sandwich effect of judging and commanding, an employee is only acting in a limited capacity. Any person taking on empowering others should understand the full threefold approach of the word.

## The first phase of empowerment

The first phase of empowerment is to build good judgement. Empowered employees don't rise from the dust. They come from a work environment rich in a number of vital qualities, and shared information is one of them. The more information employees have about the company and its goals on a daily basis, the more they feel a part of the company and the better they are able to judge what works and doesn't work for the goals of the organisation.

What information do most employees know?

### Level 1: The goals of the organisation, its history, the mission, the market.

All of this is the backbone of the organisation, and is usually given when a new employee is hired. This may or may not make sense to the new people, depending on their experience. It may or may not be true for employees, depending on the informal culture at work in Level 4.

Level 1 is the formal image of the company and not necessarily the working truth for those in the trenches. In the really empowering company, the formal and informal truth are the same thing and everyone knows it.

## Level 2: The goals of the department in which employees are working.

This is the action part of the abstract goals they learned during recruitment. Again, there is a formal and an informal part to this information.

## Level 3: The person's job description and the goals for that position.

To the extent that individuals understand their job descriptions and tasks and are empowered to do their work well, they are successful in fulfilling those jobs.

## ✳Level 4: The informal culture of the organisation. ✳

This is the level that really matters to individuals. It lets them know if they are in an organisation they can trust, one in which they can grow and spread their wings, one they can depend on, or one in which they need to spend their days protecting themselves and their turf and looking for a 'good' job elsewhere.


## Refining the art of delegation

Giving away a job can be an act of empowerment or a source of frustration on both sides. Delegation is really a matter of information sharing. The more information is shared with a person about taking on a new task, the better the result. What really goes into delegation and why is it such a problem area?

### Delegation

Delegation is still an art more than a science, in spite of the amount written about it. The art is in setting up the task ahead of time so that both supervisor and employee anticipate all the possibilities of the situation and plan for them. Delegation is certainly one of the primary ways employees understand empowerment because the quality of the instruction they are given foretells the quality of job they do.

Here is a checklist for delegating a task to someone in a way that promotes empowerment. These questions must be discussed with the worker carrying out the task to give that person a fair chance of success:

### Does the worker know enough to perform?

Always the first step is to be sure that the worker is adequately *prepared* skillwise to successfully complete the work ahead. In an empowering organisation a supervisor's job is to keep people advancing towards their greatest skill level.

### What is at stake?

The performer must know *the context* in which the job fits – the history of the job so far, any connection to other work, other departments, the scope and size of the task, who will see the finished work and what happens when it is late or not done.

### Who is in charge?

The performer needs *information* to do the task well. This includes what the finished work looks like. Without this vision the performer of the task is groping in a haze of unsaid expectations. This includes the *parameters* of the task. What gets too far afield? What needs to be checked before starting the task? This is part of creating good judgement. The person doing the task must be in charge of completing the task or else delegation has not taken place.

### When do you check back?

What are the major decision points that need to be discussed? Who will *make decisions* on large and small details? What can this person handle with good judgement and what needs a conference?

### What information does the supervisor need?

What *feedback* from the employee is needed? What information does the supervisor need to know to be informed of progress so that there is a mutual comfort level?

### How do others give their input?

*Continued support and creativity* are often welcomed and improve the final product. Suppose the supervisor has more ideas to offer? Suppose others get ideas they think would work? When can those be offered? Who decides whether they will work? Cover this information up front.

### How do they know when they're doing a good job?

What does *excellence* look like? What needs to be done at what time for everything to come together on time? What deadlines are expected? What will be the frequency of my reinforcement and on what tasks?

### How do you connect this with others' responsibilities?

Who else is *depending* on these outcomes? Whose work is waiting for signals, information or tasks completed? What happens when work is early or late?

### What help will be needed in the final phases?

What *coordination* is required in the final phases? How much help is needed? Who will do what? Who has final responsibility? Forecast and arrange for this at least halfway through the project.

### How is the quality of the work decided?

*Reviewing* the process immediately after is helpful, if not required, for the reinforcement of a job well done or correction if the job needed improvement. The performer knows how well a task was done. Start there and build on that understanding. This will tell the supervisor how well the task was explained in the first place.

## The second phase of empowerment

The second phase of empowerment is to let the employee do the task. Judgement is in place because of good information and skill level and now it's time to *act*. The job has been described thoroughly. Now the performer takes off the runway. The supervisor stands back and watches. The wings wobble a bit, the flight pattern may not be quite clear, but the supervisor stands back and watches for self-correction.

The person doing the work is the pilot. At this moment he or she is feeling a rush of triumph as well as a case of the jitters. This independence is exciting. This is also a time for pitfalls and mistakes. They don't mean the plane will crash, only that the pilot is still inexperienced. The supervisor acts as the control tower and keeps in touch, offers correction, but lets the pilot fly. The big question is, now that the plane has taken off, can the pilot bring it in?

The most important thing the empowering supervisor can do is to stay out of the way. If the supervisor constantly takes back the task or intrudes on the person performing it, the performer knows something is wrong. Either the task was not really given or it is not being done to the supervisor's satisfaction. Productivity slows, doubt rises, resentment sets in. The employee is on the way to disempowerment – a task once given turns out not really to belong to the employee, who quickly loses both interest and trust.

If the supervisor follows the previous checklist thoroughly, there should be no reason to intrude on the performer's work except to reinforce. Instead the supervisor needs to wait for the employee to share progress and concerns.

## The third phase of empowerment

Now the worker is in full flight, take-off is accomplished and we're on cruise control. But the unexpected always comes up. The worker needs to be able to respond to new situations and obstacles quickly – in short, to *command*. What does that mean? It means commanding needed resources, asking people to help, changing things that don't work. If the worker has been well trained with the needed information, good judgement at this phase should be no problem.

The best way to show this phase at work is for the supervisor to model it. The way the supervisor asks, explains, corrects, praises and thanks becomes the model for the others in the group. The better the model, the better the results from others.

The final stages of the task or project, when a number of details and threads come together at once, make up the stretch that most employees hunger for. This is their chance to keep their wits about them, respond coolly to demands and to coordinate a number of fast-breaking events at once. This is the real learning curve, where everything has been prepared for one thing: the performance.

If a supervisor or an organisation is serious about creating empowerment, they need to prepare the performer for this part of the task and understand how important it is to their growth and satisfaction level to be left alone to perform it. It is OK for the supervisor to stand ready on the sidelines, but it's not OK to begin to take over the reins, except in case of real emergency.

## Build empowerment into your day

Here is an easy way to build empowerment into your workday that benefits everyone. Remember Maslow's hierarchy of needs? (See page 20). We can use that again to show the levels of empowerment.

### Consistency
Consistency in empowerment is key to repeated performance. An organisation has to be consistent in its response to employees' attempts to grow and improve through taking risks within the organisation. This is what the 'Survival' level reinforces – a consistent welcome to employees who care enough to think for the company and risk trying to prove themselves through improving the organisation.

### Reinforcement
Reinforcement comes from knowing that, even if our flight plans are shaky or we make a crash landing, we will be assisted to strengthen them, and help will arrive to clean up. Employees who take on new tasks will be reinforced for the positive and not for the negative. In other words, we have the security of making mistakes and surviving them and that's OK. It's part of the learning experience. The 'Security' level is vital to giving a feeling of empowerment to others.

## Information

This information is 'what's *really* going on' in the organisation, the latest information about new policies and markets, new developments or products – what *people with power* know. As we saw in Maslow's third level, 'Belonging', information is the key for employees to feel as though they belong. Without it they have no stake in what is happening because they don't know enough to care.

## Permission

Permission is a factor on the fourth level, 'Prestige'. Permission is implicit in the culture of the organisation – permission to offer ideas, to discuss the need to improve methods and processes, to look beyond the immediate job towards upward mobility, to cooperate with other departments to accomplish a task faster and more efficiently. After all, when an employee's ideas are solicited, accepted and acted on, that implies respect and recognition. And that spells prestige.

## Opportunity

Opportunity can come about in three different ways:

1. Not readily available because of the non-permissive or closed nature of the culture of the organisation. The employee has to carve out opportunity the hard way, sometimes taking risks with job security since the culture does not encourage courage and creativity.
2. Offered by design by management to give employees a chance to improve themselves. This may be in the form of job training, tuition reimbursement, team projects, community outreach and so on.
3. Available by the way the organisation is run, so that opportunities for taking on new tasks or recommending changes and implementing them are available without specific invitation.

Employees implicitly know – when they have the right *information*, *permission* and *opportunity* – what can be done better and how they can assist in doing things better.

It is the information level that creates the empowering organisation. All other things can be equal, but if the real information is not shared, people don't feel as if they belong or are important and don't invest their courage and creativity on behalf of the organisation. And these two qualities are what companies need most.

## The ladder of empowerment

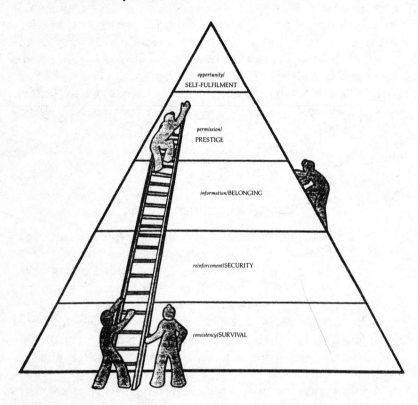

opportunity/
SELF-FULFILMENT

permission/
PRESTIGE

information/BELONGING

reinforcement/SECURITY

consistency/SURVIVAL

Maslow's Hierarchy comes into play again as we measure the climb to the highest level of employee performance. What does it take to make people excited about the organisation, loyal to it and willing to risk for it? In capitals are the traditional levels of need people try to satisfy on a daily basis. In italics are those needs the supervisor and the organisation must offer if it is serious about empowering employees to give their best.

## The empowering supervisor

The empowering supervisor holds a special place in the estimation of the workers supervised. This person knows that building people's skills makes everyone's job easier and turns out better work with greater satisfaction and less friction.

The empowering supervisor knows that every human being is a complex assortment of talents and weaknesses, strengths and fears. Under pressure of new assignments and challenges, unresolved fears and self-esteem issues can create defeat in place of victory. For this reason, the empowering supervisor is part illuminator–teacher, part cheerleader, part psychologist, part healer and guide. A simple cycle of skills will create an empowering supervisor.

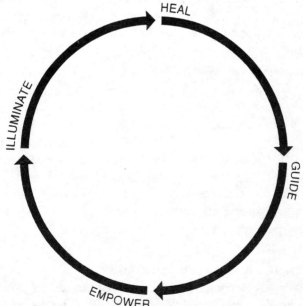

Be willing to repeat this cycle as many times as necessary with any person learning new tasks.

## The empowering supervisor illuminates

The first skill is illumination. This may seem a strange word but it is the basis of teaching. It means simply to cast light on a subject, to clarify and explain. It means to value teaching the full picture, the principles behind the task, not just action alone. Illuminating is the difference between 'giving a man a fish, and teaching a man to fish'. The person who illuminates the task and the path adds to the knowledge and skill of everyone.

## The empowering supervisor heals

The second skill is in healing. Everyone has personality traits that work and those that get in the way. The empowering supervisor knows this and works with the individual personalities to be at their best rather than getting snagged on self-defeating patterns. See page 63 in this book and review these in light of each employee supervised. Before giving someone a new task, review this information and choose your path of training. What do you need to illuminate and what do you need to work toward healing? You may wish to share this information with that person so both will understand what to look for and what needs to be overcome.

## The empowering supervisor guides

The third skill is guidance. This comes in the form of monitoring the work, reinforcing the correct choices and path and clarifying new issues and choices. Guidance is best offered in the form of questions, such as 'What will happen if you do that?' 'What do you think is the best choice?' 'What has to happen for this to be accomplished?' Always remember, better to ask than to tell. Shed light on the consequences of the action rather than the behaviour itself. People appreciate knowing consequences. They seldom appreciate being informed of their shortcomings.

## The empowering supervisor empowers

The fourth skill is empowerment. This feels much like parenting. The employee crawls, toddles, then walks. The parent stands back and watches, alert and ready but not intrusive. At any point in the task, the supervisor, if needed, goes back to the first skill of illumination and on to healing and guidance again until the staff member acts with confidence and autonomy.

## The empowering organisation

The empowering organisation is one dedicated from the top down to building leadership in the ranks. That is a stated objective at the highest levels and it is carried out every day by every supervisor. When this happens wonderful things take place. Long-term goals are reached far sooner than expected. The extra mile becomes standard and loyalty goes unbelievably high. People shine and stretch.

Here is a comparison between an empowering organisation on the right and the disempowering organisation on the left. Where does yours stand? Check the blanks for the qualities at work in your organisation. Then create plans to move right.

| | |
|---|---|
| _____ Blame | _____ Responsibility |
| _____ Information-poor environment | _____ Information-rich environment |
| _____ Fear of mistakes | _____ Love of job |
| _____ Territoriality | _____ Cooperation |
| _____ Suspicion | _____ Trust |
| _____ Protectiveness | _____ Sharing |
| _____ Lying | _____ Truth |
| _____ Cover-ups | _____ Openness |
| _____ No risking | _____ Risking |
| _____ Low morale | _____ High morale |
| _____ Absenteeism | _____ High attendance |
| _____ Low productivity | _____ High productivity |
| _____ High turnover | _____ Low turnover |
| _____ Low loyalty | _____ High loyalty |

**Become an empowering organisation**

Ideally it starts at the top. For empowerment to really work, senior executives must decide that this is what they want and then set about creating or changing behaviour patterns until they achieve it. The rewards for being in an empowering organisation are obvious to those who work there. The rewards for running one are even greater.

Any organisation that wants to be at the forefront of its industry will find itself in a constant scramble to stay in first place. The only way this is possible is if everyone in the organisation understands and is empowered to do the most outstanding work every day. No organisation in today's markets can afford to have less; yet many settle for half the productivity they could have if only the steps were taken to open up the people and let them shine.

Here is a case study of an organisation that has created an atmosphere of total empowerment:

> An insurance agent, Irene, saw an opportunity ten years ago to create an association management organisation for a large group of independent contractors. As she built the company into a multi-million pound business she set a goal to treat people the way she wanted to be treated. That means a lot of personal attention and a dedication to finding ways to reward people.

Her company offers the predictable employee of the month award, but in her company it really means something. Here is what the chosen employee receives:

- A cash prize
- Casual dress for the month
- The special parking spot for the month
- Trophy on the desk for the month
- Name on the company plaque
- An article in the company newsletter
- Name added to the list for Employee of the Year
- Lunch with chief operating and chief executive officers
- Important company news before it is announced to others.

Remember information and the way it makes us feel as though we belong and increases loyalty? Here's an example.

### Cash prizes
The employee of the year receives £500 in cash plus extra paid days to take an all-expense-paid holiday underwritten by the company. The runners-up receive cash bonuses of £250 each. Anniversary gifts are given to all employees as well.

### Lunch with the MD
All employees are invited to lunch once a quarter as managers and officers review the company's goals and project goals for the following quarter. At the lunch new awards and achievements are announced. Employees are encouraged to make short presentations to increase their speaking skills.

### Manager incentives
Managers often are promoted from the ranks of employees and learn to become cheerleaders for their employees as part of the culture of the company. They are eligible for Manager of the Quarter and receive all the perks the employees do, plus time off to attend the seminar of their choice paid for by the company. They also become eligible for Manager of the Year.

The Manager of the Year receives a return trip for two to France for seven days that includes car rental and £300 spending money.

Managers who don't work continually to increase their employees' effectiveness will find their own climb blocked because of having no one to replace themselves. They're expressly encouraged at staff meetings to talk about their employees' progress and to show how they are promoting growth and skill development.

### Suggestion box
One of the most innovative programmes in the company is the one called 'Killing the Sacred Cow' which encourages staff members to continually question the way things are done and to suggest ways to create smarter, cheaper, more efficient ways of

doing things. A suggestion box committee of non-management employees reviews all suggestions and awards up to £1000 for effective suggestions.

## Employee incentives

Not only is there a company newsletter for the association about the association, but also one about the employees who run it. This newsletter identifies the faces and personalities behind the voices on the phone and announces new faces and changes in the company. A page full of 'gotchas' mentions employees going 'above and beyond' jobs in every phase of company participation.

## The company store

The organisation has recently opened a company shop that offers items with company logos and 'experiences' such as tickets to concerts and events bought in advance and at discounts normally unavailable to individual purchasers. Employees can cash in special vouchers in the store for tickets. They can only earn the vouchers through a special point system.

The company also has a benefit package that includes free parking, profit sharing and two days' salary if no sick days are taken in a year. An on-site nursery is available to working parents. The company has also adopted a shelter for homeless and low-income children and involves their employees in Halloween and Christmas extravaganzas as well as work throughout the year.

What is in this for the company? Irene reports that each five-year goal they have set has been accomplished in as few as 18 months! Now that's empowerment in action. Any time a company goal can be completed years ahead of schedule, management must be empowering staff members and rewarding the behaviour they want.

Begin your empowerment plan on page 96.

# Part 3
# Five Steps to Success

A journey towards a productive, happy workplace begins with the first step. This section guides you through five steps which spell the acronym 'LEARN'.

*The first step is*  L earn to Lead

*The second step is*  E xamine Expectations

*The third step is*  A ct as Though You Care

*The fourth step is*  R espect Employees as Professionals

*The fifth step is*  N ever Stifle Personal Growth

Together the five steps will lead any manager to a more productive and happy workplace.

The 'L' stands for 'Learn to Lead'. That means becoming an efficient and effective time and work organiser so that you don't stand in the way of your own organisation's productivity. That kind of organised approach creates time and space for you to be with your people when you need to be and to give yourself room to grow. It's difficult to move up the ladder or try for new goals when your daily work is in disarray.

# STEP 1
# Learn to Lead

The first skill is to show *you can lead*. Do this in two ways by *being efficient* and *teaching employees to think for themselves*. A manager who is disorganised and inefficient lowers the standard of excellence and creates a state of mediocrity.

Employees respect excellence. They want their leaders to be efficient and top-of-the-line in everything they do.

What does efficient mean? It means more than just being neat. It means:

☐ being competent
☐ skilful
☐ capable
☐ and productive.

It also means *not* being:

☐ ignorant of the job needs
☐ unskilled in getting results
☐ unable to handle new situations
☐ lazy, inconsistent and inattentive.

Efficiency not only *saves* time, it *makes* time to satisfy the other levels of employee satisfaction.

## The efficient-manager checklist

Rate yourself for efficiency. Give yourself a 3 for statements you feel totally describe your situation, 2 for those that are somewhat true, 1 for any that are not very true of what you do, and 0 if the statement does not describe you at all.

_____ 1. I know the technical aspects of my job thoroughly.

_____ 2. I have organised the work flow very efficiently.

_____ 3. I control the work flow to match the way it was organised.

_____ 4. I know enough about the overall picture to relate what I'm doing to others who need to know.

_____ 5. I am personally productive.

_____ 6. I have developed tracking systems to monitor results.

_____ 7. I am neat and efficient in my work area as an example to others.

_____ 8. I can handle new situations easily when they arise.

_____ 9. I'm skilful at combining tasks for greater efficiency.

_____ 10. I encourage subordinates to suggest ideas for efficiency.

_____ 11. I am constantly on the look-out for ways to do things better.

_____ 12. I help my manager to be more efficient by anticipating needs and being prepared.

_____ SCORE

If you scored 28 to 36, congratulate yourself, you're in orbit. 19 to 27, hurrah! You're leaving the launch pad. 11 to 18, you're learning but not ready to fly. Below 11, back to 'ground school' to learn the secrets of flight.

## Employees who think for themselves

Those who think for themselves do not suffer from *analysis paralysis, boredom* or *mental malnutrition*. Train your employees to make decisions that work for them, for you, for the customer and for the organisation.

The basis of getting workers to think for themselves is to encourage them to ask questions, to listen and then offer guidance. Over time, they will learn to ask questions in order to discover answers that will serve the best interests of everyone involved.

Some sample questions which will help an employee check for understanding are given below:

1. What has to happen for this to work?
2. And then what? By when?
3. What would happen if we didn't do this?
4. Is that the result we want?
5. If not, what *is* the result we want?
6. What do we have to do to get it?
7. How does this help to reach our goal, your goal?

Add your own:

8. _____

9. _____

10. _____

A manager can't think for everyone. The basis of survival is to teach others to think for themselves.

## Bonus section: Pass on the vision

What is a 'vision'? It is a word picture describing a scene, circumstance or event. In historic times only prophets and soothsayers had visions. Today everyone needs one. Visions are road maps for the mind. They are the mark, the target towards which everything travels.

Without vision a person must depend on others for guidance. Without such guidance it is easy to wander in the dark. Organisations are the same. Without a vision of where they are going, they can flounder.

It is essential for each organisation, from top to bottom, to have a vision of where it is headed and how to get there. The organisation's vision is the goal – what it is working towards becoming. Visions are sometimes called 'mission statements'. It is the responsibility of each manager to lead others towards the vision of the organisation. Every department in every company needs to be in the process of becoming better, more efficient and more effective at what it does.

A vision, then, is a description of your mission when it is accomplished. Your job as leader is to help others.

- *See it!*
- *Want it!*
- *Reach it!*

### Share the vision!

#### Why?

Why would it be important for you as a manager to share with your fellow workers the vision towards which you're striving? Wouldn't it be easier just to tell them what to do and correct them when they miss? That used to be the way management worked. But with better informed workers who demand more participation in planning and carrying out tasks, they want to know where they're going. Why share the vision? *Because your employees can help you to get there!*

## How?

How do you share what you're trying to accomplish with others in your organisation? You can do it a number of different ways:

| *Large groups* | *Small groups* |
|---|---|
| memos | meetings |
| video announcements | on-the-spot guidance |
| training films | goal-setting sessions |
| posters | performance appraisals |
| speeches | one-to-one conversations |
| other publications | awards and incentives |

Which have you used? Which have worked? Which haven't? Why?

## Creating the vision

An organisation's vision can be split into several parts. It should explain the values a company has about itself as a business, about its employees and about its customers. The vision further describes where the company or organisation is going – the target – and how it plans to get there.

### The organisation

What are the values of the organisation? Will it be the finest, fastest, smallest, most service-orientated, most complete service, best quality or product, lowest priced, etc?

### The customer

Who is the customer and why is he or she special? How will you service the needs of the customer? Will you offer 24-hour turn around, call-out service, constant attention, self-service, white glove treatment etc?

### The employees

Who are your employees? What qualities do you expect from them? Professionals, experts, most qualified, best paid, well-trained, most polite and cheerful, best technical training, drug- and alcohol-free, etc?

## *The direction*
Where do you want to be in five years' time? Biggest in the world, 10 per cent market share, finest in the town centre, 100 outlets nationwide, etc.

## What is your vision?
As a leader, when you can accurately describe the vision of your organisation, you have established a base of understanding that can be passed along to others. This makes your organisation stronger when all members strive for a common goal.

Try describing below some values for your organisation, your customers, your employees and your direction to reflect how well you understand your vision.

*Your organisation:*

_____

_____

_____

*Your customers:*

_____

_____

_____

*Your employees:*

_____

_____

_____

*Your direction:*

---

---

Have you developed a true and complete picture of where your organisation is going? Can you describe what is important to you, what you believe in and what you are trying to create?

---

## Case study 1

How do you turn a small, struggling branch of a large corporation into a thriving, productive, profitable enterprise? Paul was given that assignment when he took over a staff of eight in a troubled division of a major organisation. Building the operation into a highly profitable unit with 250 employees took time and vision.

The eight employees initially didn't see themselves as part of a large, vital organisation. Separated by 500 miles from the main office, they worked at their own pace. They viewed their jobs in relation to the local market. Their products were good, but not better than anything else in that region.

When Paul arrived, he changed that. He made the goal of the parent company clear to each person. Paul now says, 'Everyone in this organisation knows our goals. We expect to be the best at what we do compared to anyone in the country.' He broke his operation's goals into three areas:

1. A profitable rate of growth
2. Develop new customers and service existing ones in a superior way
3. Train employees to accept personal responsibility for productivity and profitability.

'Everything we do, every decision we make, we measure by those three points. And I do mean "we". All employees are involved in decisions that affect their productivity.'

---

The next letter in 'LEARN' is 'E' for 'Examine Expectations'. Too often it is an easy matter to hire people to fit a job that works well on paper but does not fit the human spirit.

The Industrial Age made great use of 'human assembly lines'. That philosophy has changed as people have become better informed about motivation. During this same period employee expectations of job satisfaction have also risen greatly.

This second step shows you how to provide security for employees by examining and matching your expectations of their jobs against theirs.

# STEP 2
# Examine Expectations

Two factors managers often overlook are that people like to see the end result of their efforts and they enjoy work when it is interesting. Amazingly, these two aspects are often undervalued.

Examine the expectations you have for your employees. Do you expect them to put out a high level of productivity if they don't feel involved in the end result? Are they bored doing the same task over and over again? Do you accept that boredom is a primary ingredient of their job? Do you feel that allowing them to see the final outcome is unimportant?

When workers don't see the end result of their activities, it is hard for them to get excited about what they do. It is hard for them to feel any ownership in their work. In fact, the smaller the role a worker has on a given project, without positive feedback, the less that person feels like improving his or her output.

When you involve workers and explain their responsibility as it relates to the end product or service, then they know what to expect. Knowing what to expect gives most people a desire to contribute. Not knowing makes too many of them non-caring and ineffective – feelings that create low productivity.

## Reorganise the work flow

Sometimes, simply rearranging the flow of work will boost productivity. Studies have shown that almost any attention paid to the flow of work will have a positive effect.

One successful manager moves equipment and work stations and reorganises duties regularly. She is willing to experiment to achieve greater efficiency. The employees help her in planning the moving of equipment.

The key point here is that the employees are involved in the decision-making process. Questions such as 'What would work better?', 'How can we get more out of this situation?', 'How do we reduce the noise level?' help the workers to focus on improved productivity and come up with their own solutions.

One assembly line worker did the same repetitive task for 17 years. When the work flow was rearranged to give him total responsibility for customer contact, problem solving and follow-up, his productivity went up 40 per cent.

Take a close look at the work flow arrangement in your area of responsibility. What could be done to change it for the better? Ask some questions of your employees. Get them involved with answers and plans.

## Make work interesting

The second need at this level of employee satisfaction is to make work *interesting*. Workers who do primarily only one thing all day, every day, quickly become bored.

To guard against boredom there are several things you might consider. These include rewriting job descriptions, rearranging work flows, giving more responsibility for problem solving, providing recognition for a job well done, etc. Loosen up and liberate the potential of the people working for you and you will be rewarded with improved morale and higher productivity.

Mark yourself with these statements:

_____ I regularly discuss decisions with my employees.

_____ Employees are comfortable giving me their opinions and advice.

_____ I listen to employees' comments, consider them and provide feedback.

_____ We often make group decisions.

_____ I make sure my employees feel involved with the end product.

_____ I make sure they understand the vision towards which we are working.

_____ I give employees authority to make meaningful decisions.

_____ I hold employees responsible for their decisions.

_____ We have developed a system in which we all profit from good decisions.

_____ I constantly check to see that pace, variety and involvement in work are designed to maintain high interest.

_____ SCORE

---

Give yourself a 3 for always, 2 for sometimes, 1 for once in a while, 0 for never. If you scored between 23 and 30 you've taken the lid off your people's potential. At 16 to 22 your people are ready to grow. If between 9 and 15, paralysis is taking over. Below 9 you have created some zombies.

---

The next section provides a guide to problem solving. Problem solving not only makes work interesting, it helps workers to see the result of their efforts. Ownership of problem solving pays off. Interest runs high, enthusiasm increases, morale goes up. People feel they help to control the outcome.

## Bonus section: SOS - Solution finder

### Situation + Opportunity = Solution

*Here's the Situation.* Your staff are very busy. They're working full out every day. Each Monday morning you conduct a staff meeting. During meetings people are needed to answer phones and attend to other details. To miss these meetings is not to know what's going on. No one has been taking minutes. Since some of the material is confidential, it can't just be posted up. There has been no established method for getting good information from the staff meeting to those who can't attend.

*Here's the Opportunity.* Now that we've described the problem in detail, it's time to look at the opportunity. We can redesign the communication flow through new responsibilities, new work flow, new scheduling, and increase team spirit at the same time.

*Here's the Solution.* Brainstorm among your staff for as many different solutions as possible. *Put down a minimum of 20 ideas.* This will force the group past some obvious answers into something more creative. Then assign responsibility and deadlines for putting the plan into action. Use the form on the next page to organise thoughts. By the way, how would you solve this situation?

1. **Situation.** Describe the situation in *detail*.
2. **Opportunity.** State your goal in positive terms. Describe the outcome you would like to see achieved.
3. **Solution.** Brainstorm 20 possible approaches to achieving the goal. Then choose the best suggestions and organise into action steps.

Action step 1. _____ Date to initiate: _____

Action step 2. _____ Date to initiate: _____

Action step 3. _____ Date to initiate: _____

Action step 4. _____ Date to initiate: _____

Responsibility to coordinate:

_____

Deadline for completion:

_____

---

## Case study 2

Morale and productivity were low when Shelley took over as administrator of a county office. The office had received bad publicity from the local newspaper for a situation where the management had lacked foresight and effective follow-up. Her employees were defensive and bored.

Shelley decided to change the atmosphere by reorganising the work flow among her staff. Some had not done any different tasks in years. She asked them to help her design new information systems. They did. She made sure they got out of the office to see the end results of decisions.

Shelley then met the editor of the paper and showed him that bad publicity was really counter-productive to both their needs. He toured the office and asked many questions to understand the situation. He arranged for a more positive story about changes that had been made since the critical articles appeared.

When some of the employees were recognised in the newspaper for good work, she wrote each person a note of congratulation. A once dead office began to thrive again.

The next letter in 'LEARN' is 'A' for 'Act as Though You Care'.

When employees feel they come first with their manager, customers will feel they come first with the employees. It's much easier to give when you are receiving. As managers listen, respond, and care for their employees, the employees do a better job of caring for customers. Managers' behaviour becomes reinforced in a self-perpetuating cycle.

# STEP 3

# Act as Though You Care

To make people feel they belong, there is no better way to show an attitude of caring than by getting them involved and then listening to their comments.

Show you care by *listening*. Listening to employees when they have ideas on how to do things better is one of the most important things managers can do. Companies that listen normally get higher productivity and excellent two-way communication. They create the climate for bottom-up suggestions that get heard, used and appreciated.

When employees are not asked for their opinion, or worse, asked but not taken seriously, they become disconnected from the vision. They don't participate in the future of the organisation in the same way as others. Being listened to is one of the most important ways people contribute to an organisation. If that is denied, they lose interest and turn their energies to other things.

## Learn to listen

Here are some guidelines for listening to employees:

### Treat them as professionals
They'll be more likely to respond professionally if that is the attitude conveyed.

### Ask how they see the situation
Take notes if necessary, but ask questions that give you as much information about their view as possible.

### Make no value judgements
Listen, nod and make notes and stay neutral until they have finished. Don't add opinions like, 'You know that won't work'. Concentrate on the information in a friendly way.

### Reply as soon as possible
People like to hear an answer – even a polite 'That won't work in this situation because ...' – or at least a progress report of what is being done. Otherwise they feel left out, overlooked or unimportant – all feelings you want to avoid.

### Consider the 'hidden' message
There are sometimes other messages behind the information employees provide – a need for recognition, a desire to blame others, criticism of management, etc. Listen to what is not being said as well as what is being said.

### Provide follow-up opportunities
Use the SOS approach to create solutions.

## Keep employees informed

The other side of the belonging level of satisfaction is to *keep your employees informed*. Without information they can't know what's going on. They won't know what progress is being made towards the organisation's goals and won't know how to help make things happen.

It is natural to feel left out when information is lacking. Just as when not being listened to, employees can feel unimportant, overlooked and undervalued if they do not receive regular feedback.

Often when employees don't get enough information or are not listened to, they form subgroups to manufacture their own information. These are called 'grapevines' or 'cliques'. Instead of spending time and energy helping to achieve the objectives of the organisation, they create diversions.

When employees in any subgroup are left out, the employer loses both productivity and commitment. The organisation suffers.

Listening to and informing your staff is one of the greatest ways to close the commitment gap.

**A listening and informing survey**
How important is 'belonging' as a success factor to you? Take the self-test and find out.

Give yourself a 3 for absolutely, 2 for some of the time, 1 for once in a while, and 0 for never.

| **Listening** | **Informing** |
|---|---|
| Be honest with yourself about your listening style. When employees discuss work items with you, how well do you listen? | How well do you inform your people? When employees want to know what's going on, what do you do? |

_____ I know the value of listening for the morale of my employees.

_____ I know the value of keeping employees informed.

_____ I listen to all members of my staff as one professional to another.

_____ I give equal information to everyone who needs to know.

_____ I obtain the necessary details from each conversation.

_____ I prefer to inform employees in person rather than by memo.

_____ I make no value judgements while listening.

_____ I create time to inform.

_____ I create time to listen.

_____ I make it a point to update those who are absent.

| Listening | Informing |
|---|---|
| | |

### Listening

_____ I know the value of listening to the success of my job.

_____ I reply as soon as possible when a reply is required.

_____ I coach others in listening skills.

_____ I listen for any hidden messages.

_____ I provide follow-up and an opportunity for solutions.

_____ I'm a good listener.

_____ SCORE

### Informing

_____ I informally share information to help others on a regular basis.

_____ I include all involved personnel when new developments occur.

_____ I withhold as little information as possible.

_____ I use information to help get everyone excited about the job.

_____ SCORE

TOTAL _____

---

A score of 51 to 60 shows your ears and mind are open! 41 to 50 means you're doing a solid job. 31 to 40 means your people often feel left out. 21 to 30 suggests a real problem. Open your eyes, ears and mind.

## Bonus section: Your unique style

Belonging means feeling appreciated. An employee needs to feel that his or her unique qualities are appreciated. When this occurs, it increases a feeling of belonging. People who appreciate one another tend to view themselves as part of a team. They share ideas, values and goals.

For over 2000 years, four basic personality types have been recognised. Hippocrates first described them in 400 BC. The names have changed and information has been added to Hippocrates' original description, but the four types have stayed basically the same. Although each of us tends to be more of one type than any other, we have some of all types in us.

Hippocrates named the personality types after various fluids in the body: 'choleric' for hard-driving and impatient individuals, 'sanguine' for happy-go-lucky types, 'phlegmatic' for slow moving, steady souls, and 'melancholy' for those of us who are sensitive and introspective.

Today the types are often called driver or dominant, inspirational or influencer, analytical or steady and compliant or amiable. Which type are you?

## Four personality types

In each square below you will probably see yourself. But wait. Choose the square that is *most* like the real you!

| **The Pioneer** | **Wheeler Dealer** |
|---|---|
| *(choleric)* | *(sanguine)* |
| Pusher, Producer, imPatient, Powerful, Persistent, exasPerating, to the Point, unPredictable, comPelling, Problem solver, OverstePs Prerogatives | Debonaire, Dashing, Devilish, no Detail, Delightful, aDaptive, iDea person, Democratic, non-Dictatorial, Desiring to help and please, Diplomatic, Dynamic |

<table>
<tr><td>

**Captain Caution**
*(phlegmatic)*
Caretaker, Conservator, Keep
the balance, Consistent, Kind,
Careful, Calming influence,
Cooperating, Concise,
Conventional

</td><td>

**Systems Thinker**
*(melancholy)*
Sensitive, proceSSor, need
Sensor, Stage manager,
Synergist, Systematic,
Supportive, Synthesiser, Self-
critical, Standardised,
Sympathetic

</td></tr>
</table>

## Which personality type are you?

Which type is most like you? _____

Which is your next strongest style? _____

Which is least like you? _____

For fun, see if you can list selected associates, employees, friends,
etc with their primary style.

| *Name* | *Most likely style* |
|--------|---------------------|
| _____ | _____ |
| _____ | _____ |
| _____ | _____ |
| _____ | _____ |
| _____ | _____ |
| _____ | _____ |
| _____ | _____ |

## What each personality type needs to be effective

Regardless of personality type, each person requires a different approach by a leader to give their best. No two types should be treated the same. It is part of the leader's job to learn how to handle each personality type to get the best performance from everyone.

**The Pioneer Needs:**
- lots of challenges
- correction when needed
- to be shown *what* you want
- some prestige
- an opportunity to learn new skills
- a feeling of competence

**Wheeler Dealers Thrive On:**
- democratic guidance
- lots of people contact
- plenty of variety
- a good time
- public recognition
- being told *who* is on the team

**Captain Caution Wants:**
- a stable environment
- to be shown *how* to do
- encouragement of analytical talent
- plenty of warning before change happens
- to be probed for real feelings
- economic security

**Systems Thinkers Like To:**
- create harmony
- to be shown *why* it's done
- use a detail approach
- avoid criticism
- be given praise in private
- have time to process information

## When under stress

Everyone responds differently to pressure. Each personality type acts in a certain way when the going gets tough. Understanding this behaviour will help a leader to avoid problems. The following are some reactions common to each type. Realise that any individual may not show all of these.

| The Pioneer Says: | Wheeler Dealer Says: |
|---|---|
| 'I'm in charge here.'<br>'I'm bored and restless.'<br>'I don't care, I'm doing it anyway.'<br>'I can't stand routine.'<br>'I'd just as soon work alone.'<br>'To get it done quickly, I'll do it myself.' | 'I want everyone to love me.'<br>'I don't care, I'll give my heart.'<br>'I've changed my mind today.'<br>'I love you all; you're great.'<br>'I don't have time for facts.'<br>'Wherever has the time gone?' |

| Captain Caution Says: | Systems Thinker Says: |
|---|---|
| 'Don't rock the boat!'<br>'I can't seem to get going.'<br>'I like things just as they are.'<br>'Tradition is good enough for me.'<br>'I'm waiting for my orders.'<br>'I don't care, I'm not changing.' | 'It's not my decision.'<br>'There's no rule about this.'<br>'I'll have to look it up.'<br>'I don't care, I didn't do it.'<br>'Let's get more information first.'<br>'I can't change until you tell why.' |

### What's in it for you?
What is your pay-off for recognising and dealing with the different personality styles? Mainly, your life as a leader and manager will be much easier if you stop struggling with different styles and adapt to them instead. You can help your people to be their best by giving them work that is most appropriate for their style.

When you encourage each one to be 'their style':

**The Pioneer Becomes:**
- a risk taker
- a decision maker
- an independent worker
- an agent for change
- a results-orientated person

Other _____

_____

_____

**Wheeler Dealers Turn Into:**
- inspiring leaders
- diplomats
- enthusiastic workers
- favourable impression givers
- contributors of high morale

Other _____

_____

_____

**Captain Caution Contributes:**
- steady work
- patient approach
- being a loyal employee
- following instructions
- being task orientated

Other _____

_____

_____

**Systems Thinkers Provide:**
- specialised skills
- details
- high standards
- careful decisions
- a high level of accuracy

Other _____

_____

_____

### How to use the styles

Though we each have a dominant or 'home' style, our challenge is to use the other styles when they are desirable. The more versatile you are, the greater your options will be.

As a manager or leader, you know that one thing you have to do is to push for results, plough new ground and explore different paths. This brings out the *pioneer* in you. When you need to be a pioneer, become comfortable with those qualities and use them.

Once you've found the right path, you need to be more interested in people. These individuals need to be led, using diplomacy and tact. Bring employees together to reach the goal you've mutually established. That's the time to be a *wheeler dealer*. Your ability to influence and inspire will help to get the job done.

As you develop people to become productive, you need to develop some routines. You're still using your first two styles, but now the organisation and maintenance phase requires task-orientated skills. You have to watch expenses, work flow and morale. You become more like *captain caution* during this phase.

Now it's time to standardise the progress you have made, so you call upon your detail-orientated characteristics to make sure things are done properly. You become analytical and control results as a *systems thinker*.

## Case study 3

Joe is supervisor of a large group of retail clerks. From experience he has observed that each person has a unique style. Joe has learned that it is easier to capitalise on a person's style than to fight it.

'I quickly recognise how each person prefers to work,' he says. 'You can tell during the interview. I watch how they fill in the application and how they respond to questions.'

Joe takes time at the beginning to observe how new employees respond to information – how they act on it and work with it. Then he assigns tasks according to styles.

'If I want something done fast, I call on Maureen or Ron. Both move like lightning, overcome problems and deliver results quickly.'

People like Ralph or Trudy who like to work on details, get a chance to do just that. The talkative, outgoing ones such as Sue and Rob are trained to handle special problems such as customer service and new product sales. Those like Dan and Rick who are better at projects than dealing with people are put to work organising new systems and streamlining procedures.

By staying aware that everyone has some of all styles, Joe works to balance each person's style with new challenges. His people appreciate his sensitivity to their uniqueness.

The next letter in 'LEARN' is 'R' for 'Respect them as Professionals'. As you begin to appreciate the value of the individual to the success of the organisation, you create a more respectful environment. Upgrading the workplace with fresh paint, more light and artwork is always a good idea.

Attractive surroundings are a good way of showing respect, but more important are the ways in which employees are treated in their daily duties.

People instinctively know when they are treated with respect and when they are not. Respecting your employees is a value that needs to be addressed with every meeting, with every act you make as a manager.

Step 4 will give you an opportunity to analyse how well you offer respect to your fellow workers.

# STEP 4
# Respect Employees as Professionals

Two of the most important things a manager or leader must do are to *treat people with respect* and *offer recognition when earned*. You know from your own feelings how important these two qualities are in making people happy on the job.

No matter what else is going on, if workers do not get *respect* and *recognition*, they will eventually be unhappy and unproductive.

It's not enough:

- to be an efficient manager
- to teach others to think for themselves
- to show employees the end result of their work
- to provide interesting work
- to listen; or
- to inform

Employees must also feel respected as individuals and recognised for good work. Respect can best be shown by treating employees like professionals. Hire them professionally,* talk to them as professionals, and when the going gets tough, ask opinions professionally. When you provide a professional atmosphere, employees will feel and respond accordingly.

---

* For more information on interviewing, read *Conducting Effective Interviews* (Kogan Page).

## Respect employees' feelings

Respect and recognition communicate the worth of an individual. When you communicate respectfully, you are saying, 'Your feelings are important to me'.

Respect is free. It needs to be consistent. You've created a position that requires someone to give an honest day's work in return for your honest day's pay. When you put a person in that position, it is essential that you respect that person's ability to do the job.

You can show respect – or the lack of it – in a number of ways. Mark yourself on the following. Give yourself a score of 3 for always, a 2 for some of the time, a 1 for occasionally, a 0 for never.

_____ I greet each person pleasantly each day.

_____ I take time to manage by walking around, ask questions, chat and listen.

_____ When I talk with employees, I make eye contact and speak respectfully and pleasantly.

_____ I include them in as many decisions as possible.

_____ I ask for their advice on matters concerning their job, work area or other related items.

_____ I treat everyone equally.

_____ I do not withhold information from any team member.

_____ I call employees by their preferred name.

_____ I do not assign an overload without including essential employees in the decision-making process.

_____ I emphasise team spirit.

_____ I do not assign special projects without carefully analysing the growth needs of my people.

_____ I praise in person when a job is well done.

_____ I correct in private on a job not well done.

_____ I offer coaching to improve job performance and new skills.

_____ I insist on high standards and communicate that respectfully.

_____ SCORE

If you scored 37 to 45, your people feel highly respected; 30 to 36, your folks feel all right; 22 to 29 they feel you don't respect them very much; 15 to 21 a revolt is brewing.

## Recognise quality performance

We all love positive recognition – that wonderful moment when someone important lets us know how good we've been.

When we know we've worked hard and earned that moment, _we want it!_ Without it, we feel short changed, unrewarded, and unvalued. Our spirit droops, the energy goes out of us, our pace slows.

Never underestimate the power of recognition as a motivator. It's the oil that keeps the machinery turning. Studies show that people work harder for recognition than for money.

That's why recognition needs to come both formally and informally. It must also meet these important points:

1. Recognition must be given in a way that treats every person and effort equally.
2. It must reward for true accomplishment, not superficial or momentary gain.

3. It must fulfil the goals of the organisation, the customer and the employee.
4. It must guide and encourage the worker.
5. It must be done in a positive and public way that encourages others to strive for the same.
6. It must be done informally as well as during a formal time of recognition.
7. Other: _____

_____

_____

_____

**A time for you!**
In case you feel recognition is flowing more from you to other people than the other way about, take a moment to recognise your good work. List below some of your best efforts in the past week, month and year. Add any personal acts that made other people feel good about themselves. Include off-the-job deeds, too.

This week I'm proud I did:

_____

_____

_____

_____

Within the last month I'm proud of:

_____

_____

_____

_____

Within the last year I'm proud I was able to accomplish:

_____

_____

_____

_____

*Hurrah for me!*

## Bonus section: The power of [4]

Part of getting and giving an honest day's work is realising how important people are to the success of any organisation. As we realise this, we change from thinking of them as tools and concentrate on growing them as resources.

Growing people is like planting a garden. To produce a good crop you start with healthy plants, provide the best start possible and nurse them carefully. If you were to tend your people as carefully as you would tend a garden that was your own source of food, what kind of crop would you get?

Organisations are not only about making money. They are about growing the business, growing profits (or reaching the goal) and growing people at the same time.

You need four elements to grow good people. Together they are called the power of [4].

### Synchronised energy
The power of the four elements shown below produces enormous energy. The total power is truly greater than the sum of

the parts. Create these four elements and learn to harness them for a powerful workforce.

### The power of [4]

| | |
|---|---|
| **VISION** | **CHALLENGE SKILL DEVELOPMENT** |
| **A SENSE OF BELONGING** | **FUN** |

These four elements of an effective workplace add up to a whole that is greater than the sum of its parts. These four factors create *synergy*.

### Synergy = synchronised energy

This closes the commitment gap!

### The fun factor!

The single element getting the most attention from the power of [4] these days is the fun factor. Enlightened leaders are beginning to realise that enjoyment and work go together. It is an excellent way to develop self-esteem, skill development and a sense of belonging.

The great 'people motivators' have fun with their team. They have it both while working hard and sometimes by playing hard. They use fun as grease to turn the wheels a little faster while the machinery is running hard and to lubricate it while it is resting.

Research has shown the healing power of laughter when people are ill. Research is also showing the motivating power of

---

Adapted from Warren Bennis and Burt Nanus, *Leaders: Strategies for Taking Charge*, Harper & Row, 1985.

fun while working hard. You want an honest day's work? Have some fun!

Fun doesn't have to be expensive in time and money. It can be part of the job. It can be as simple as an attitude. Fun usually falls into the following categories:

1. The fun of new skills;
2. The challenge of being the best;
3. Taking time off for fun on the premises; or
4. Having fun together off site.

---

## Case study 4

As a business owner, Joanne has always been a hard worker. She has owned a beauty salon for 15 years and has 12 people working for her. She has fun with her employees, yet works at being the best salon in the area. Her idea of fun is to be first with new styles and techniques. She rewards hardworking employees with paid trips to shows in national exhibitions where they learn the latest news in the hairstyling world. Do they socialise after work? Definitely, including an outing in the summer and an end-of-year party. The rest of the time they have fun at being the best.

Patrick is a manager for a large computer company. He has a sales force of 25 people and spends time with each one. He gives lots of 'strokes' for good work. Patrick notices little things his team does well and comments accordingly. He is high on recognition and the sales force seems to thrive on it. After exceeding major sales targets, Patrick arranges fun events such as theme parties or treasure hunts. Whatever it takes to achieve a feeling of belonging to something special is something Patrick is willing to do. No wonder he has been consistently recognised for superior sales performance over the years.

The next letter in 'LEARN' is 'N' which stands for 'Never Stifle Personal Growth'.

The last step on your climb to motivating your people to give their best is to create opportunities for personal growth. Without that the lid is on tight. People stagnate and languish. When you have provided the other four levels of employee need, keep on going.

The great pay-off for encouraging growth among your employees is that you, as manager, will inevitably grow. If you spend your energies controlling people and keeping them from growing, you have no energy left to grow. On the other hand, when you create growth for others, you create it for yourself.

Step 5 gives you the opportunity to measure your IQ – your Innovation Quotient. Like all the other self-assessment quizzes in this book, this one is designed to provide you with guidelines for new management techniques.

Congratulations on a successful climb. After you finish Step 5, create a celebration for yourself and your staff!

# STEP 5

# Never Stifle Personal Growth

The last step to successful people management is to *give employees room to grow*. The greatest satisfaction workers will have in the future will be to find a challenge in their work and develop new skills.

The world is changing faster and faster. An employee's only hope to keep up with it is to grow in understanding and skill development. Your job as a leader is to provide that opportunity.

If you remember, *interesting work* was one of the first points covered in this book. Even if work is interesting, it remains that way only to a point. It is then your job to provide more challenge and skill development.

There may already be a high level of challenge and skill development in your work. If so, congratulations! However, remember that all levels need to be satisfied for people to be happy.

It's up to you, the leader, to create an atmosphere of innovation. This means you open your own mind to new and better ways of doing things and then open your workers' minds to the same.

## How high is your IQ?

How do you create a spirit of innovation? Check your IQ – your *Innovation Quotient*. There are people who criticise what's wrong, people who suggest better ways for others to do things, and people who find a better way to do them. Which category are you in?

Take this quick self-test to check your Innovation Quotient. Score 3 for always, 2 for sometimes, 1 for once in a while, 0 for never.

_____ 1. Are you a sleuth? Do you look under the surface of what's going on – problems, trends, feedback from others?

_____ 2. Are you an 'innovation opportunist'? Do you find opportunities for solving problems, creating wants, filling needs?

_____ 3. Are you a strategist? Do you spend time redefining your goals, correcting your course and revising plans to reach them?

_____ 4. Are you a challenger? Do you examine assumptions, biases, preconceived ideas for loopholes and opportunities?

_____ 5. Are you a trend spotter? Do you actively monitor change in your field, such as technology, politics, or attitudes, to spot opportunity early?

_____ 6. Are you a connector? Do you keep your eyes skinned for concepts you can borrow from one field and apply to another?

_____ 7. Are you a risk taker? Are you willing to develop and experiment with ideas of your own?

_____ 8. How's your intuition? Do you rely on your true feelings?

_____ 9. Are you a simplifier? Can you reduce complex decisions to a few simple questions by seeing the overall picture?

_____ 10. Are you a need filler? Do you look for the human need behind statistics?

_____ 11. Are you a visionary? Do you think further ahead than most of your colleagues? Do you think long term? Describe your vision to others?

_____ 12. Are you resourceful? Do you dig up research and information to argue your case? Do you use information creatively?

_____ 13. Are you a listener and feedback junkie? Do you look forward to hearing from others about your blind spots? Do you welcome better ideas from others?

_____ 14. Are you an innovation networker? Do you have lots of contacts with whom you communicate to share thinking, get excited about a new approach or idea? Do you seek out other innovative thinkers?

_____ 15. Are you a futurist? Are you fascinated by the future?

_____ 16. Are you a reader? Do you devour books, magazines, articles that deal with success stories, innovation in general, in your field of interest in particular?

_____ SCORE

A score of 41 to 48 shows you paused just long enough in your pursuit of a vision to answer these questions. We'll see your name in lights some day. 36 to 40 shows you're ready to step up to team playing with the 'discoverers'. 30 to 36, you're awake and willing and a good support person. Below 29 you're a maintainer and conservator of the past. Your talents seem to lie in other areas.

# How high is your organisation's IQ?

An innovative organisation breeds innovative people. Take a look at your work atmosphere:

_____ 1. Is innovation highly regarded in your organisation?

_____ 2. Is innovation built into the strategy of your organisation?

_____ 3. Is innovation implemented quickly?

_____ 4. Do you have a meeting to discuss opportunities as often as you have one to discuss problems?

_____ 5. Are your reporting systems set up for qualitative as well as quantitative information?

_____ 6. Do you staff innovative processes with your best and brightest people?

_____ 7. Do you always keep before you the purpose of your product or service?

_____ 8. Do you have a think tank?

_____ 9. Do you celebrate innovation with ceremony?

_____ 10. Are innovators treated like heroes?

_____ SCORE

A score of 24 to 30 indicates an organisation which highly values and rewards innovation. 17 to 23 deserves a 'well done'! You're alive, awake and enthusiastic about developing your people. 10 to 16, rev up your motors to catch up! Below 10, arthritis is setting in. You're moving too slowly to keep up in the market and keep good people.

## How do you do it?

How do you foster innovation in your organisation? You need to develop a positive attitude*, a commitment and some ground rules.

### *Attitude*

- You need an attitude that encourages openness, curiosity, willingness to experiment.

### *Commitment*

- You need to commit to innovation as a value in the vision of your organisation.

### *Ground rules*

You need to develop the following:

- Flexibility
- Openness about feelings
- Fairness
- Fun
- Detachment – some ideas don't work
- Encouragement.

## How does your garden grow?

If you are innovative but your organisation is not, how do you encourage your people to bring out their innovative tendencies? Give yourself a 3 for yes, 2 for sometimes, 1 for occasionally, 0 for never.

\_\_\_\_\_ I help them to set goals for new skill development.

\_\_\_\_\_ I celebrate any progress with them.

\_\_\_\_\_ I reinforce points along the way.

\_\_\_\_\_ I send them out of the office for growth experiences.

---

* Read *How to Develop a Positive Attitude* (Kogan Page).

_____ I keep them posted on new developments in their field.

_____ I encourage them to read and take courses.

_____ I create time for my personal skill development.

_____ I create challenges for them.

_____ I value their input.

_____ I spend time discussing opportunities with them.

_____ I foster brainstorming sessions.

_____ I recognise innovative performance.

_____ Other _____

_____ SCORE

---

29 to 36, you're a leader as mountain climber. 23 to 28, you're a great burden bearer on the trek. 15 to 22, you'll do as base camp support. Below 14 – you missed the boat. You are vegetating.

---

## Bonus section: Your score sheet

Take a moment to record your scores from the previous self-assessment pages in this workbook:

1. Are you giving the top ten? (page 23)  SCORE _____

2. The efficient manager's checklist (page 45)  SCORE _____

3. Make work interesting (page 54)  SCORE _____

4. Your listening and informing survey (page 61)  SCORE _____

5. Respect employees' feelings (page 72)  SCORE _____

6. Your Innovation Quotient (page 80)  SCORE _____

7. How high is your organisation's IQ? (page 82)  SCORE _____

8. How does your garden grow? (page 83)  SCORE _____

YOUR TOTAL SCORE: _____

Of the possible 312 points, if you scored over 250 consider yourself a superior leader. Over 200, a very good leader. Over 150, on the right track but need help. Under 150, more training is needed to make you an effective leader.

Now that you've completed the five steps to motivating your people, it's time to set some goals.

As you know, goals are meant to help you get where you want to go. Set some goals now to help you attain the five levels of employee satisfaction.

## Goal setting ... start here!

Begin your development plan by analysing the most important level of need for each employee. Check off the satisfaction levels of each of your staff. Leave blank those qualities you think need attention. A 1 is survival, 2 is security, 3 is a need to belong, 4 is prestige and 5 is a need for self-fulfilment:

| Name | 1 | 2 | 3 | 4 | 5 |
|------|---|---|---|---|---|
|      |   |   |   |   |   |
|      |   |   |   |   |   |
|      |   |   |   |   |   |
|      |   |   |   |   |   |
|      |   |   |   |   |   |
|      |   |   |   |   |   |
|      |   |   |   |   |   |
|      |   |   |   |   |   |
|      |   |   |   |   |   |
|      |   |   |   |   |   |
|      |   |   |   |   |   |
|      |   |   |   |   |   |

With each employee begin to supply the lowest level of need first. If Joe is missing both survival and self-fulfilment needs, survival will be more important. Prepare a plan for filling that need and mark off time on a calendar to prepare a plan, create conference time with each person and follow through as needed.

## Your development plan

Go back to page 23 and record your score for each element. Colour in from left to right how far you are in each one. For instance, if you gave yourself a 3 on efficiency, colour all the way across. If you gave yourself a 1 or 0, colour in appropriately.

|  | 0 | 1 | 2 | 3 |
|---|---|---|---|---|
| 1. I am an efficient manager. | | | | |
| 2. I encourage them to think. | | | | |
| 3. I show the end results of work. | | | | |
| 4. I offer interesting work. | | | | |
| 5. I listen to employees. | | | | |
| 6. I keep them informed. | | | | |
| 7. I treat them with respect. | | | | |
| 8. I recognise and praise good work. | | | | |
| 9. I offer challenge. | | | | |
| 10. I encourage skill development. | | | | |

Now you know where to begin to increase your effectiveness as a manager and leader. On the next two pages outline your plan for improving your performance and reaching some of your own goals.

## Aim for the top

| 1st goal | 2nd goal | 3rd goal | 4th goal |
| --- | --- | --- | --- |

### Step 1: What do I want to accomplish?

| | | | |
| --- | --- | --- | --- |
| | | | |

### Step 2: What is keeping me from it?

| | | | |
| --- | --- | --- | --- |
| | | | |

### Step 3: What knowledge, skills and abilities do I need?

| | | | |
| --- | --- | --- | --- |
| | | | |

### Step 4: Whose help do I need?

| | | | |
| --- | --- | --- | --- |
| | | | |

| 1st goal | 2nd goal | 3rd goal | 4th goal |
| --- | --- | --- | --- |

*Step 5: What's in it for me?*

| | | | |
| --- | --- | --- | --- |
| | | | |

## Continue your climb

| 1st goal | 2nd goal | 3rd goal | 4th goal |
| --- | --- | --- | --- |

*Step 6: What sign will I look for that I'm reaching it?*

| | | | |
| --- | --- | --- | --- |
| | | | |

*Step 7: What are the first steps I need to take?*

| | | | |
| --- | --- | --- | --- |
| | | | |

*Step 8: What comes after that?*

| | | | |
| --- | --- | --- | --- |
| | | | |

| 1st goal | 2nd goal | 3rd goal | 4th goal |
| --- | --- | --- | --- |

### Step 9: What do I do if things go wrong?

| | | | |
| --- | --- | --- | --- |
| | | | |

### Step 10: What's the earliest/latest possible completion date?

| | | | |
| --- | --- | --- | --- |
| | | | |

## Case study 5

It's not easy to provide challenge and skill development unless it's written into your plan. Time slips by and systems work well enough so new skills sometimes seem a luxury a leader can't afford.

Diane, a head nurse in a drug and alcohol rehabilitation unit at a metropolitan hospital, creates time for her people to sharpen their skills.

No matter how heavy the load, she insists her nurses take the necessary time to study their new patients' cases. That way they can be completely prepared and professional during the first meeting. She also sets aside lunch time on a bi-weekly basis to discuss news in the field and encourage ideas on how to do things better.

Diane makes sure her staff attend seminars that motivate as well as educate them. She sees her staff as a close support system for each other, as well as for the patients. Their spirits need constant refreshing because of the intensive nature of the work. 'I know how important the stimulation of new skills is as well as the need for quiet time for planning and preparation. A constant demand on energy and skills without replenishment is no fun and eventually destroys effectiveness,' she says.

# Part 4
# Practise What You've Learned

## Touch their hearts

Each level of employee satisfaction and each quality therein touches the nerve ending of a vital need. Remember that as you go about your work as leader and manager.

Every manager touches the needs of each employee every day. As a manager you can ignore these needs, manipulate them for your own ends, or fulfil them for the satisfaction of all – including customers and others in your organisation.

Choose to fulfil your employees' needs. Your life will be richer and freer. Your own climb will be that much higher as you bring out the potential within your people. Give them what they want, and they'll give you what you want.

Touch their hearts and they'll give you theirs. Aim for the heart.

## Two-week checklist

**Date    /    /**

It's easy to read and file this book. You may nod knowingly as you look over the pages and think, 'I knew that'. But unless you make a commitment to follow through, you will not have closed your own commitment gap to better leadership.

To avoid losing the impact of the points covered in these pages, get started today. Two weeks after reading this workbook, check your progress by completing the following exercise:

\_\_\_\_\_ I have started to increase my leadership skills.

\_\_\_\_\_ I have incorporated my goals into a daily and weekly plan.

\_\_\_\_\_ I have scheduled time for each employee on an informal basis.

\_\_\_\_\_ I have listed the needs of each employee and begun to work on a plan.

\_\_\_\_\_ Each plan is incorporated into my calendar so that I make sure I do what I committed to do.

\_\_\_\_\_ I have concrete goals so that I know when I'm making progress.

\_\_\_\_\_ I give myself respect and recognition when I complete each new task.

\_\_\_\_\_ I'm on my way to being a 'superior leader'.

## Three-week checklist

**Date** \_\_\_ / \_\_\_ / \_\_\_

\_\_\_\_\_ I can now give the top 10 qualities (page 23) to my employees and get an average score of 25 or better.

\_\_\_\_\_ I have incorporated all 10 points into a standard operating procedure.

\_\_\_\_\_ I am on my way to liberating the potential of my people.

\_\_\_\_\_ I also notice a difference in my own performance.

\_\_\_\_\_ I aim for the top when I work with people, not just my staff, but everyone.

## One-month checklist

**Date** / /

\_\_\_\_\_ I have traced the three reasons the job doesn't get done.

\_\_\_\_\_ I have rearranged the work flow as needed.

\_\_\_\_\_ I have shown my employees the end result of their work.

\_\_\_\_\_ I have varied the pace and variety of their work for interest.

\_\_\_\_\_ I am sensitive to respecting their needs.

\_\_\_\_\_ I have begun to encourage people to think for themselves.

\_\_\_\_\_ I offer recognition by _____

_____

\_\_\_\_\_ I've created a think tank for greater creativity.

An empowerment plan is sketched out on the next page. Use it!

## Your empowerment plan

The goal of this planning worksheet is to gradually move the tasks from column one to two to three.

| | Supervisor decides, does | Employee recommends, does, has checked | Employee decides, does |
|---|---|---|---|
| Task 1 | | | |
| Task 2 | | | |
| Task 3 | | | |
| Task 4 | | | |
| Task 5 | | | |
| Task 6 | | | |
| Task 7 | | | |
| Task 8 | | | |
| Task 9 | | | |
| Task 10 | | | |

Use this page first as an assessment tool. If you're a supervisor, ask yourself how much empowerment you have given to each particular employee. If you're an employee looking for more independence, use this as an assessment sheet for yourself and an entry point of dialogue with your supervisor. Good luck and keep moving from left to right.